The Grace of God in Action

The Grace of God in Action

GOD'S GRACE IN ONE MAN'S DEATH MARCH

Pastor Valentine H. Derr

VANTAGE PRESS
New York

Cover design by Susan Thomas

FIRST EDITION

Copyright © 2004 by Pastor Valentine H. Derr

Published by Vantage Press, Inc.
419 Park Ave. South, New York, NY 10016

Manufactured in the United States of America
ISBN: 0-533-14752-2

Library of Congress Catalog Card No.: 2003096674

0 9 8 7 6 5 4 3 2 1

Contents

FROM HOME TO TENNESSEE

Introduction and Narrative

Hello, my name is Valentine Derr. I was born on January 7, 1919. Among millions of others of the Depression generation, I was called upon to go to war for our nation. Many have told their stories of those days, and I think it's time that I should tell mine. Mine is no different from many others. Many people suffered more in their service than I did. Many were in the Japanese prison camps where barbarous treatment cost them their lives, and others were in death marches. And I praise God for what He did for me.

As I get older, my memory for these things seems to come fresh in my mind. I have difficulty remembering four things to bring from the grocery store (that my wife asks for), but I can remember sharper now things that happened fifty-eight years ago when I was captured in the Battle of the Bulge.

1 Uncle Sam Doesn't Want Me

I was inducted into the army in 1942. I had graduated from high school in 1936 and was fortunate to have a job for the six-year period. Like others, I signed up for the draft. We were given a number, and my number was drawn in the first half hour of the fish bowl drawing in Washington—in the beginning of the draft. I've forgotten the exact year.

However, I had had a problem in my mouth. I had teeth that needed attention, and I had a double row of teeth that came in. In those days, we didn't have the skills that dentists and dental surgeons have today. I couldn't get anything done for a long time. So when I went through my physical examination when they did call me, the doctor reported all that he found, and they deferred me. And I started a job in a locomotive shop for a steel mill.

My girlfriend and I were talking about getting married. We decided, when I was deferred, that we would get married. Now, I need to tell you something before I go on. While we were going together and among other things, I was active in my local church. I felt the call to go into the Christian ministry, and I talked to my pastor at that time, because in Findlay, Ohio, our denomination had a college, which had what they called the Ministerial Course. Since I was deferred, I thought, *I'll go, if we can work it out.* I asked my pastor if he could get me some information. He had an important office in our conference, and he was in Findlay many times.

However, things didn't work out at that time. We did get married on August 17, 1941. Time went on, and later, in 1942, I found a dentist who would work on my teeth. So I got the teeth fixed.

2 *Disappointment and Rejection*

My boss at work asked how long I would be off work, so I told him what the dentist told me, that it wouldn't take more than an hour, so I would only be off one day. Unfortunately, in the process of cutting of part of my upper jawbone, he cut an artery, and I bled profusely and became very nauseated and weak. They did not give me a transfusion and sent me home in two days.

It took two weeks until I had strength enough to return to work. I had only been on the payroll three months when this happened. Furthermore, I was hired because of my experience with high-speed diesel engines that the people I worked with didn't possess! I knew before they hired me that "the new kid" on the block who is different from his peers is not quickly accepted; in fact, however "the new kid" tries to meld with the group, he can never be one of them. The men I worked with were much older and had worked together for many, many years.

I found myself in just this position when I returned to work after my absence, and there were personal problems about how I went about some of the jobs I was asked to do that made hard feelings that made me feel like an outcast.

After about three weeks, I told my boss on a Tuesday that the coming Friday would be my last day and that I would need a pass to take my tools past the guard station. So on Friday I left.

3   *Uncle Sam Wants Me Now*

At this time there were many jobs around, so I figured I would go out the following week to look for a new job. As I remember, I think it was Wednesday of that week, I received a notice to report to my Draft Board—even before I had looked for a job. The job I quit was considered vital to the war effort, and I am sure the personnel department of that corporation called my Draft Board on the Friday I left. The Draft Board gave me orders to come to their office on July 2, 1942, for induction into the United States Army. At the Draft Board office, they put a whole group of men on a bus and sent us to the Army Induction Center at New Cumberland, Pennsylvania.

4   *In the Army Now*

I reported to the New Cumberland Induction Center on July 2, 1942 and was sent from there to the 80th Infantry Division, 305th Combat Engineer Battalion, Company "B" at Camp Forrest, Tennessee. Our basic training involved seventeen weeks rather than the thirteen weeks that the infantry got, because we also learned how to build bridges, demolition, removing and laying mine fields, doing river crossings, building floating bridges, and all the things that went with it. Our training started at the end of July 1942, and it ended at the end of November. My wife had come to join me while I was there, and she had a room in one of these large, Southern mansions—places where people rented out their rooms to servicemen's wives. I was allowed to spend two nights a week off the army post and weekends, unless I had duty.

5 Possible Changes

In the beginning of 1943, I had been promoted to the rank of Sergeant. I went into camp one morning after leaving my wife's room—on a bus that came every morning—and that day, the Company Commander was there. The Charge of Quarters said (when I came into the company area)—that the Company Commander wanted to see me. So I reported to him and he said, "I'm here early this morning, because I wanted to talk with you and several other men whose wives are here." He said, "We're forming a cadre, to go and organize and make a new division in the army."

I asked, "What's a cadre, sir?" "Well," he said, "No, you don't know what that is." He told me, "They will take about sixteen hundred non-commissioned officers from the 80th Division here, and they will go to a new place where they will start to train inductees as they arrive." And he said, "There are two lists. Although I don't know which list the army will select, and I don't know where they will be going, I thought you may want to send your wife home."

6 Change and New Organization

Well, we had a son who was about to be born at that time, so it was well that she go home to have the baby. Even if I hadn't gone, that was a good idea. As fate would have it, I was on the list that the War Department selected. And in due time, we left the 80th Division, went to Fort Jackson, South Carolina, to form the 106th Infantry Division. There we were in the 81st Combat Engineer Battalion, Company B, attached to the 106th Division. The division was formally activated on the fifteenth of March 1943. We began our training program as we moved in there as the inductees came in.

It was my understanding, and it seemed to work that way, that the emphasis was on younger men going in the division to have special training so that when it went into combat, men would have had thorough training against some who were just men who came with hardly any training to put into combat immediately. Well, that worked for a while, but when the 106th was about three months on in its development (as I remember), they started taking replacements out. I remember that for a while, I was the supply sergeant in Company B of the 81st Engineers, and it was my responsibility to see that they had all the clothes and everything that was to go with them. And I got the first thirty ready to leave there and go to the replacements.

7 *Army Duties*

And then sometimes some came in who were quite young. We had some from many different places. But basically that was the principle. These men who came originally were from college, universities—seventeen, eighteen-year-olds, and at the time, I was twenty-four years old, and the sort of looked up to me. And I got to know all of them, being the supply sergeant, I knew all their names. I saw them come and go. Now we stayed in Fort Jackson, South Carolina, and we continued to lose some—not so many at a time, and then others . . .

8   To Tennessee for Maneuvers

The division moved out on the twentieth of January 1944 to Tennessee maneuvers for additional training as nearly like real combat as feasible. We came off the maneuvers in March 1944. And when we came off there, they sent us to Indiana—to Camp Atterbury—twenty-five miles south of Indianapolis. We stayed there, and the Army, again, came in and took more men, and they took officers with them. They had sent a small cadre out from the Engineer Battalion. We were short of officers, and they were a little while in replacing them. I was Platoon Sergeant, Third Platoon, B Company.

For several months during the summer, I had no commanding officer, and as we were going through our training just the same, we spent a lot of time in the field in that camp. In the latter part of the summer, I did get a commanding officer—lieutenant assigned to the platoon. As the year 1944 wore on, some of our division packed up and left Camp Atterbury.

9 *Family Goes Home*

If I remember correctly, some of the artillery and some of the infantry went to someplace—I didn't know where at the time—and my wife and my son were with me in Camp Atterbury. I was fortunate in picking up an old car—a Lafayette Coupe. The tires on it were badly worn, and I became an expert on changing and repairing tires and tubes. And I had the privilege of spending time with them after duty hours, reporting back in the morning for reveille. We heard about the Normandy invasion, June 6, when we were at Camp Atterbury. Toward August, I said to my wife, "I think that they're soon going to send us somewhere, because part of the division has gone, and maybe they're going to send us someplace else." I took my furlough and put everything in the car that I could for our son, who was just a toddler at the time, and shipped the rest. We came back to Pennsylvania. We made it safely in spite of seven flat tires on the way. God surely was with us. I sold my car, and my wife and son were safely at home.

10 Move to Camp Miles Standish

I returned to Camp Atterbury, and the Eighty-first Engineers stayed until about September, or along in there—these dates are not fresh to me, exactly. They sent us to Massachusetts, up to Camp Miles Standish. We discovered when we got there that some of our artillery—the ones who had left Atterbury before we did were already there. It seemed like they were massing the division around that area. We still had training up there, and we were there about a month. Being combat engineers, we had a lot of men who were carpenters, and we had time to build part of a barracks for the folks there at Miles Standish.

As the cold weather came on, they limited our off-post passes; we could only go thirty miles, because at any time they might call us. I went into Providence one Sunday, on a Class "A" pass, I think it was, and when I came back, in our barracks, the men were all packing up. I asked "What's going on?" They said, "We're shipping out tomorrow." So I packed up my duffel bag and all that went with it, and the next morning we got on a train there, and they took us to the Boston Harbor, where we got on the liner—the *Wakefield,* which had been the *Manhattan,* a liner that took people on tours around the port of New York. It had been fitting for troop-carrying. So on the tenth of November 1944, we sailed out of Boston Harbor, one miserable, rainy, cold night.

14

11   *God's Continuing Presence*

What I'm trying to do by telling my story—I want to reveal the times that I, as a Christian, believe that God's grace was at work in my life. Now I cannot say I know what God is going to do. But as I look back over these things, I see numerous times when I probably wasn't aware of it, but something unusual happened.

12   *Across the North Atlantic*

So I want to share this with you. As I sailed out of the harbor that night, I had these thoughts (and I'm sure that many men had these and many others): I wondered if I would ever come back to see my homeland again. I wondered if I would come back on a stretcher or on a hospital ship. I wondered if I would be buried in a foreign cemetery or blown apart—whether I would be there a long while, whether my son would remember me because of his youth—all these things went through my head as I watched the marker lights go by us when we went out the channel. We traveled without convoy, and somebody said that there were eight thousand men on the ship. There possibly were.

13   *By the Grace of God*

We arrived in Liverpool, England, seven days later. First day out, we had run into a North Atlantic storm, and I thought that ship was going to sink! It rocked and rocked. But anyway, it was a pretty good ship, and it made it through. When we arrived at Liverpool, we unloaded our material and went to a place near where Shakespeare had lived—if that's anything of interest to you—there was an air base there, and the bombers came in and out over the place where we stayed.

14   We Go to Europe

We were only there a short time, because on December 1 (or the second—I don't know), we sailed on LSTs (Landing Ships intended for Tanks). We had picked up some new trucks there that were replacing our older trucks that we left in the United States. We rode in these down to the south of England, got on LSTs, and we sailed across the English Channel to LaHavre, France—the mouth of the Seine River. We bounced around there in the Port of LaHavre, for a day or two, and then we finally did get clearance (or whatever we needed) to sail up the Seine River, which passes Paris, to a place called Rouen, where, if you known any Christian history, they burnt Joan of Arc.

15 Convoy to Our Destination

And we got off the LST there—they dropped the gate at the front. We drove our trucks off, and we went up to a field there, where we pitched our tents in mud. The next morning, the field was a sheet of ice. I don't remember whether we were there two days or one day. But we left, and we made a short trip to some little place—I've forgotten the name of that—and I think we stayed there a day. We started north the next day, through Luxembourg, to Belgium, and it was a cold, wet, snowy, rainy, miserable trip all the way up. We finally got to the border of Belgium. We went past a town called St. Vith. We didn't know then that it was a prime target—that particular city—because of its rail and highway—transportation/road center that the Germans needed for what they were going to be doing a few days after that.

16 We Made It

We went through there, and we continued on, for approximately five miles, to a town called Schonberg, Belgium, on the Iore River. The river—yes, it might be a hundred feet wide. But it had a bridge over it, and it had houses there. We were sent there to relieve the Second Division Engineer Battalion. The Second Engineer Battalion was getting ready to go for R&R. The Army orders (I learned later) said that when we went in there, we were to relieve them, man for man and gun for gun. They would leave, and we would take their place.

17   Settling In, Looking Around

Now we had a little chance—for a couple days there—we arrived on December 10, I recall—to talk with them as they got ready to move out. This had been such a quiet place, that they said, "You've got a good spot. Nothing has happened here for months!" As a matter of fact, the Second Engineers had time to go out to houses that were damaged or blown up, and gathered up the good lumber and material—and they were able to build a mess hall! They had lights in it, and they said that the only action around there, sometimes—the Germans would roll in a railway gun and fire a few for just for effect—to let them know that they were still there! So they said, "You've got a good spot!" Well, that was good news.

We relieved them, on or about the tenth of December, after our convoy trip up from France. They certainly had pushed us in there in a hurry.

DAYS OF BATTLE AND SURRENDER

18   Final Instructions

There was a dirt road that went up a hill, over the river bridge into Germany. Now this was part of the Ardennes Forest. This hill wasn't extremely high, but it was about three-quarters of a mile from the river up to the top of it. This road continued over the top of this hill, down the other side into Germany. We were in Germany when we crossed the river. And down toward the German Siegfried Line, past an abandoned German town called Bleialf.

On this road, also, was an intersection at the top of the hill where there was a large stone house. If you were to go up the hill from Schonberg, you could make a left turn onto this road that went along the crest of the hill. The army called it Skyline Drive. It had been there before the war. The Second Engineers told us, whatever we did, we were not to send three trucks up there and have them make a left turn onto Skyline Drive. They said the German artillery had that point all zeroed in on with their 88s. They said, "You have to get around that corner fast, but if you send three trucks, two of them probably will make it. But the third one would never make it." So that was one thing that we were not to do.

Our mission, when we got there, was to pick up where they left off. So we moved into the houses where the Second Engineers were living. They had found a stove there, and that made it a little bit more comfy inside with the stove, as there was lots of wood around that we could burn. So we moved into those rooms, and as soon as we got in and were settled, we started about our primary mission, which was to maintain the roads. This was an immediate need, because the roads that went back through the valleys of the

25

Ardennes Forest led to where our infantry was up in those hills. They had replaced the Germans who had been driven out earlier in the year. They needed supplies and rations. So we needed to take care of those roads. They were mostly dirt.

We started our work in earnest there on the fourteenth, and we worked there all day on the fifteenth. And then we came back, and of course, we didn't work on them at night. And on the sixteenth, we went out to work in the morning—sent the trucks out after we had breakfast in the mess hall. We worked all day on the fifteenth, and came back that night and had our evening meal and were sitting around talking, or some playing cards and stuff, finally going to bed, and the fires in our stoves going out—ones we had covered up.

About four o'clock that morning, one of our security guards whom we had out walking around—one of my men from the Third Platoon came in. He woke me and said, "Hey, Sarge, wake up!" I asked, "What do you want?" He had a flashlight, because the only lights we had in the room were a couple of candles. So he lit a candle, and I asked, "What time is it?" He told me, "I brought this in to show ya." In his hand, he had a piece of shrapnel. He said, "This landed near me about fifteen feet! A while ago." He said, "It was cherry red when it landed—it was so hot! So I waited till it cooled off, and I picked it up to bring it in to show it to you." He said, "They've been shelling the town all night!"

19 The Enemy Reveals His Presence

I got up right away, I called the other fellows, and I told them to get everybody up. Our lieutenant had another room nearby. I sent word over to them, and we all got up. That morning, the cooks got up and started to make breakfast for us. We thought maybe we might have to do some fighting that day. The only thing—when we went in the mess hall and had our breakfast, nothing had happened to do any damage to the town yet. But they were still shelling. After breakfast, we sent our people out in the trucks to go out and work on the roads, because we had no word about anything else.

20   *Preparing to Deploy*

Usually my lieutenant and I went out in our jeep—we had a jeep driver—to the work areas. It left a space in the trucks and stuff for carrying some more material out to the road. Just before we were ready to go—I'm ahead of the story! Our jeep driver went on sick call that morning, and he had left earlier to go back to the medics—he and a couple of the others.

Just as we were getting ready to go out after our men, the Charge of Quarters came out. He said, "I have a message on the telephone in here from Division Headquarters. They want to talk to a commissioned officer." My lieutenant was the closest one there. He went in and took the call from division headquarters. The message was, "Be prepared to deploy your entire company to help stem a small breakthrough." Now this was the first we knew there was more coming. So he said, "Well, we'll have to get the trucks turned around."

And they had been gone about twenty minutes, and there wasn't a lot of traffic coming toward them, so they had made pretty good time out through there. So I said, "Well, the only way we can get there quick—we'll go up and we'll go around the corner up there by Skyline Drive, and go out there and take that crossroad that goes around the other end of the area that the infantry is in. We'll get them turned around to come back." So we did that.

And we did get them to come back. The road on Skyline Drive was all full of shell holes where artillery had landed. I was dodging around them all the way out. Safely, we made it—by the grace of God, there! And we got them back to

Schonberg, and we loaded some up who were there—some men who were still back in Schonberg, because everybody hadn't gone out—we gathered all the company. So we all got in our trucks, crossed the bridge at the Oire River in Schonberg, up the hill, to almost the top. The company commander had received orders as to where we were to deploy our men. So we went up this hill—almost to the top. There we deployed our men.

21   *Preparation and Frustration*

Now, I need to tell you just a little bit about the 106th. After they had taken a number of men out of the 106th to go over across the sea somewhere for replacements—to the Pacific or Europe, we didn't know—we got men from the Special Training Program that the Army had for men who had never seen a rifle or had one—while we were at Camp Atterbury, we had to train some of them, and we hadn't a whole lot of time.

We got fellows from the paratroopers—who had broken legs or something and couldn't jump anymore, and we had a short time from the time we got them in Camp Atterbury to get them assimilated into the division and training. But I must say this: when we went up there, the day that I had to deploy these men, the lieutenant told me what he wanted, and that is in my mind every day. Every day of my life for the last 57 to 58 years, I see this time. I see these men that were younger than I was—not that I was that much older—they called me "Pappy." But anyhow, it was hard to put them there, because although that was my duty, they hadn't seen as much of life. It was just hard to do. But we had to do it. There was no choice. But it has remained in my mind, and I'll talk about this later.

Anyway, we went up without a round of ammunition. Every man had a rifle, every man had a weapon of some kind. We had machine guns, but we didn't have a belt of ammunition. We didn't have a round of ammunition for our rifles. My weapon was a carbine, and I had no ammunition for it. We had .50-caliber machine guns, and no ammuni-

30

tion. We had bazookas, which fire rockets that will destroy a tank, but no ammunition. No hand grenades. And we went up to meet the enemy.

22   *A Small Bit of Action*

Now, the day had worn on, and about 10:30 or 11:00, our battalion commander and a senior warrant officer, who had been in charge of each company's clerk, where all our records for each company were kept, came up himself. He and the colonel came and brought enough ammunition that we got two belts of machine-gun ammunition for each platoon. Each platoon had one .30-caliber machine gun. We got five rounds for each rifle, and most men carried the rifles. I got ten rounds for my carbine. We didn't get anything for the .50-caliber machine gun, and no rockets at all for the bazooka.

We had some action after that. The enemy, and fortunately, they got there at such a time that we were able to stem the advance, and the advance first were Volksgrenadiers—infantrymen. They were older soldiers—foot soldiers, and we repelled them.

After noon it seemed to settle down for a little bit. Then it started to snow again. It had snowed before—again, it started to snow. And in the afternoon, there was a little bit of activity, not much more, but we did get a lot more snow. Then we saw some men on the other side moving around in white uniforms (so that they could camouflage themselves). We held out till night; of course, they shelled us all day long. Shells and mortars were coming over us, screaming meanies all day—coming down through the trees, and we could see limbs fly off and come down through there—and little fires start someplace because they hit some dry wood.

23   *Search for a Better Place*

Anyway—we were able to evade that, on the night of the sixteenth, which was Saturday when it began. My company commander sent my lieutenant and two men out to see if they could scout for a better place, if the darkness would make it possible for us to find a more strategic place to make a defense. We didn't have enough of anything to be offensive, and the offensive force was four to one. Four of them and one of us. And this was our first experience with combat. And these men whom we had worked fine at what they were trained to do. They did everything they could in the right way. So on this scouting move that my lieutenant and the two men were making, they ran into a German patrol. They threw a grenade in front of our lieutenant, and he was blinded. And he had shrapnel in his legs. And he couldn't walk. So we practically dragged him back to our position. That night, we moved back a little and helped him along until we found a place where the company commander thought we would hole up for the night. It was pretty well sheltered, and we had a pretty good field of fire.

24 *Moving Down the Hill*

So we stayed there overnight, and in the morning, we noticed that we could move down the hill just a little more and have even a better position. So we moved there, and as we moved, we were moving down this hill that we had gone up, and we were getting to the end of the tree line. And as we moved, we carried the lieutenant on a blanket that we had found. There had been a reconnaissance company beside us when we moved up there on that Saturday morning, and they pulled out later that morning. They left a lot of stuff behind. So we found a blanket there, and we were carrying the lieutenant, and trying as much as possible to keep him warm. We did the best we could to make him comfortable.

Next morning we moved farther down, because there was nothing we could do anymore. The company commander made an inventory of how many rounds of ammunition we had. I had one round left, and some of the men had none out of the five they had had to start with; in fact, we didn't have ten rounds. It was a good thing we didn't have more action that day—the Grace of God again. We moved down this hill to a sheltered place. The company commander drew us all together, and he said, "Now, if any of you want to leave—if you think you can make it on your own and somehow or another sneak through the woods to catch up with some American soldiers, you are free to do it. There will be nothing done—no court-martial for it or anything else." Well, nobody left; we continued there; we moved down the hill.

Now we reached the line of the trees, and we couldn't hide anymore. We noticed, as we moved down, there had been a grassy area before, but it was all full of snow now—two feet deep in places. Our air force couldn't help us because the sky was overcast, clouds were hanging low, and they didn't know where we were. They didn't have communications between the ground and the air like they do today. So anyway, we noticed that across the Oire River, which was down from us on the mountain, that the bridge at Schonberg had been blown out, that there were some of our trucks standing on the road—apparently they were sent back early and never got across because there was no bridge. And there were trucks that we could see in Schonberg from up there that were in the town. We could see from there that the wheels were shot up under some of them.

By this time, we were out in the open as far as there were trees and cover. Also, we noticed across the river, there was a German patrol. German soldiers over there—we could see that they had an armored scout car, and I don't know—there were several cars there. Between the river and the road to Schonberg that also went back to St. Vith, which I mentioned earlier, that there was enough space there—a little meadow—between the road and the river—and they were on this meadow there, watching us go down. Now, some of them must have already been over there, because they came over to meet us.

25   *Find a Litter—Wade through Our River*

As we were going down, carrying the lieutenant on the blanket, we stumbled over something in the snow. We reached down. Here, it was a litter, like the medics use. So we asked the guard if we could put him (the German guard who had come over to meet us)—could we put him on there?

Well, yeah—that was all right. So six of us picked him up and were carrying him down the hill on our shoulders through the snow and everything, approaching the Oire River again. And as we got down there, there was only one way to cross the river, and that was to wade across it.

Now this river was draining the water out of the Ardennes Forest, and there had been a lot of snow. This had been, again, Germany's coldest year in fifty years. And the men waded across, and the six of us waded down the river, and it was very swift and cold! As we got to the far side of the river—the water was only up around my waist—and the first few men got to the far shore. They got out of the water and put the little legs of the litter on the meadow. And then the next two hopped out. And I was on the downstream side of the last two. And I told the man above me, "You hop out, and then I'll crawl out." So just as I was to make my last step, before I climbed out, I stepped in a hole in the bottom of the river. And, of course, my hands were very cold. And it caught me by surprise, and I lost my grip. And immediately the stream started to take me with it.

26 *I Lose My Grip—Go with the Stream*

I noticed there was a German officer on the shore. Some of them wore blue overcoats, even out in the combat area. He had his blue overcoat and black boots on. He had a burp gun hanging over his shoulder. And when he saw me go with the stream, he started to run! Now I could see downstream a distance—I don't know exactly how far it was—maybe eighty feet or ninety feet—something like that—where there was a little bit of ground jutting out into the river.

Apparently, the river made a turn there. And when he started to run, he called to me in perfect English, "Try to work yourself to the shore!" I said, "Yessir!" And, "I'm trying." I had a wool uniform on; I had a sweater, I had my field jacket, I was soaked to begin with, and I was trying to struggle. I couldn't touch the bottom sometimes, because the stream would push me if I tried to get closer to the shore. Finally, I did work my way over. And I could see him downstream as I was approaching him. He walked out on this little piece of land that jutted out into the river. And I saw him take his boot and stand on it to see if it would be solid enough to hold him. Apparently it was, because he walked out on it as far as he could. And when I got there—I said the stream made a turn—well, it sort of swept me along with it. And when I got close there, he said, "Give me your hand!" He was holding his hand out. So I got close enough. He was able to reach me, he got my hand, and he pulled me out of the water.

That kind of flabbergasted me. A German officer who would reach down and do that. The grace of God, again! That has run through my mind time after time after time af-

37

ter time. It's the grace of God that this happened. Could he have been an angel? Angels are spoken of many times in the Bible, and they take many forms. Could they take the form of this officer? What did God want with me, anyway?

But anyway, he pulled me out of the water, and when he got me up on solid ground, he said to me, "That must be very cold." I said, "Yessir, it is." I couldn't see his rank until I saw him standing up. We have to accord their officers the same recognition as we do in our army. I said, "Yessir, that's very cold. If it would be any colder, I think it would be dry ice."

And he said, "I want to ask you a question. But first I want to tell you something." He said, "Now I'm not an intelligence officer. We know who you are. We know what your strength was to begin with. We know what happened with you. We knew the situation you were in. There was nothing you could do. You were overwhelmed." "Yes!" I said, "That's true. We were."

And he said, "I'm not going to interrogate anybody or anything like that. Because that's not my job. I'm a field officer—to do as called for my rank and everything." He said, "What I want to do: I'd like to ask you a question."

I said, "Well, sir, you have the upper hand. You're certainly free to ask me a question. I'm hoping I'm able to answer it."

He said, "You can." He asked, "What state are you from?" I said, "I'm from Pennsylvania."

"Ohhhhhhhhhhhhhhhh!" he raved! He said, "That's a beautiful place! Pennsylvania is very much like Germany! In so many places!"

"Yes," I said, "From what I've seen of Germany, it is. Rivers and lakes and forests and all these things of nature. Yes, it is very much like it."

He said, "Well, I'm glad you're at least out of the water. Let's walk back to your men."

I said to him, "May I ask you a question?"

"Yes," he said.

I said, "Evidently you have traveled in much of Pennsylvania."

"Yes," he said, "Much of it." As we talked, we walked, and he said, "Go back to your men, and good luck."

27 We Become Prisoners of War

His men were standing around. These men all had weapons. And one of the things that has gone through my mind—he had a lot of options open to him. He didn't have to pull me out of the water. He could have just shot me, in fact. He had a pistol hanging over his shoulder. They were shooting prisoners. That went through my mind. Then he could also have let me go, and maybe along the line somewhere, somebody would have seen me go by, and be a target and shot me or let me drift on somewhere—I don't know. He could have told one of his men to shoot me. Or he could have just driven away and taken everybody else and let me stand out there. The grace of God was at work right there again. So after we gathered with our respective men, he said, "I have to turn you over to somebody else." I said, "I understand."

There were forty-eight of us there from Company B of the 81st Engineers, without weapons, along with our company commander, and my wounded lieutenant (whom they put in a command car and sent away—he recovered his eyesight, and I saw him after the war).

So there were other German soldiers there who marched us away.

TO 12A . . . COMMUNION AT 12A

28   *Now We Are Prisoners of War*

We came to a Belgian house—it was occupied by the farmer who lived there. They put us in his basement—all forty-eight of us—and put our company commander, who was also with us, up in a room of this farmer's house. On the next morning, December 19, they got us out. Since action started on the 16th—it was now the 18th when we surrendered, and we hadn't had anything to eat or drink that whole time—that's not unusual. That happens. But anyway, there was nothing to eat that morning. (Later, we discovered this period was an omen of things to come.) So they got us all out of there, and out in front of this house—the "A" Company of the Eighty-first Engineers had blown a big crater out there, at a road intersection, that the Germans, if they were going to pass by and use the road, would have to either go through it or go around it. It was in a place that was difficult even to get around. So they had to go through it.

Their little bugs—little Volkswagens and Opels—they were hanging up in it, because it was deep, and there was mud and snow down in it. They first of all made us go down to help push them out of there. Other cars came along, and Ford trucks came along; they made us start to fill this hole. We'd have been there two weeks if we'd ever filled it up by hand. Our company commander came out, and he told the leader of those people that this was against the Geneva Convention. You cannot put prisoners to work in a combat zone.

We still worked for a while, and then they decided after they had looked back of this farmer's house, where he had a whole pile of saplings back there—about an average of three inches in diameter. They were fairly round and about ten to

43

twelve feet long. I don't know whether they knew we were engineers or not, but we do, as combat engineers, build a road called a corduroy road. It's logs tied together—usually very close to the same diameter—and as round and straight as you can get them, and then a lot of times we'd tie them together so that they wouldn't shake apart. It's a good way of getting across mud and obstacles.

The German sergeant who took charge of this took me back of the holes, and he said, with his finger—we couldn't understand each other, but I understood what he was saying—"Lay them side-by-side." Okay. I said, "No." He said, "Yeah! . . . Yeah!" so he took his pistol out. "Yes!" Okay. So we went out and started to do that, but as we were carrying these out and laying them side-by-side (I knew they wouldn't stay there), I said to my men, "Don't pick out all the straight ones." Quietly, on the sly, I said, "Pick out some of those dog-legged ones and put them in."

So we'd take some of them, and he would stand there ranting curses because we were putting them in. I said, *"Nixferstain* [I don't understand]!" We'd walk away from him, and then they'd pull them out, and we'd put them back in again. But as the trucks came, they'd get stuck in the mud, and we'd make like we were pushing them, as they wanted us to do. And all the time we're holding it back and making their wheels spin more and more until we quit having so much mud all over us. Finally, somebody came down in a vehicle, and some officer came over and talked to this man. He told us, "Go. Go!"

Some other German soldiers came down after this—in a truck—after this car came down with officers. They came over with their rifles and stuff, and started us up a road that went away from there—up a hill. There was no place to go. So we started out and up this hill, and more prisoners started to come with us from an area that we had not seen, where there had been a terrible battle—we saw dead men, blown up—vehicles everywhere—as we walked away from this place. And there were whole streams of men coming from there. They joined us, also. Soon the road was full of American prisoners of war. We looked and saw our company commander at this time, never to see him again. He did survive the war and was later living in New York City.

At the top of this hill, there was a town called Prum. It was only about three miles from where we had been. And somebody from Lancaster County, Pennsylvania, could speak and understand enough of this German. He said they were taking us to a railhead. They were going to put us on a train and send us to a prison camp. We got up there to the top of the hill at Prum, and there was no train there. The Air Force had been in there and had blown all the railroad tracks out. So we walked on.

That same day, as near as we could figure, we walked about thirty miles. Now we were still in pretty good shape, even though we had missed some meals. We were still in pretty good physical shape. So that night, they put some of us in a barn, and then there were so many there that they took the ones who were in the barn—it was snowing again—and they put us all out to stand around the field. We still had our steel helmets. And standing out in this field of snow like the cattle gets pretty tiresome; the cold starts to work on you after a while. And we had been cold now for a long time. We weren't even warm in that Belgian cellar! That was damp!

So next morning, we started to walk again. And there were some men there with us—there was one man who had a big wound in his muscle on a lower leg. And it was bleeding, and it was a good thing it was wintertime, because it froze some of the blood and stopped some of the bleeding. And incidentally, I never saw that man again until we were

45

freed in a place that was under American control. And he hadn't had it treated yet.

Now let me go on with my story . . .

We walked about another twenty-five miles, and I don't know how many of us were in that column when we finally got to a place called Gerolstein. When we got there, we went to an immense warehouse that was totally empty—there was nothing in it. It had concrete walls—of course the floor was concrete. And there was nothing to eat. There was nothing to lie on unless you wanted to lie on the concrete. And most of us did, because we were so tired and wet and so worn out, that we just lay on the concrete.

The next morning when we got up, they opened the door on the side of this building, and they counted us—each one of us—as we went out the door. Now outside the door was a boxcar. A train of boxcars was standing out there. It was on a curve, and you could see the locomotive out ahead, and a whole stream of cars when you came out, you could see these. They counted sixty-six of us and put them in a little French boxcar, which was intended by the French army—that the Germans just took and kept—were good for forty men or eight horses. With sixty-six in there—we were so tight we could not sit down. We had to stand up. And there was no place to sit. We were just like sardines in a can. They gave us a little bit of something to eat that time. There was a little biscuit—like maybe a quarter of an inch thick, like white dough or something—about the size of an Oreo. We had two of them in a little wax-paper-like bag. And they had some caraway seeds in them. That's all there was. No water. Nothing else.

As the cars were filled, they were locked shut, and the train was moved forward to the next one, and they kept putting sixty-six men in, until the entire train of boxcars was full. Now there were men—soldiers form the 28th Division Pennsylvania National Guard, and from the 99th Division, the 4th Division—lots of us from the 106th and many others. This was our baptism of fire—our first combat. Our first incident. We did with what we had in the position where we were ordered. Green as grass. But we were there. By the grace of God, they didn't shoot us. Because Hitler had ordered, there were no prisoners to be taken.

So after a while, the train finally was filled, and we started out. We crossed the river. We were in Belgium for just a short time, and then there was a sign at Koblenz; we went into Germany. We traveled for about three days. After three days, the train pulled into a railroad yard, and then backed this train on a siding, down the hill from a large building up on the top of the hill. The whole train was on the siding. Between the train, this big wall of ground beside us up to this big building on the top—was a distance of about thirty feet. The guards were out there all the time, and the cars were locked shut. There were no sanitary facilities—nothing. We were kept in there. By this time, all of us had diarrhea, because some of the water—I forgot where we got any—what we had of it was tainted, and carried a lot of bacteria. And we were in there on the 23rd of December.

About 7:00 P.M. it was dark, of course—a British plane came flying over. How do I know that it was British? One man was familiar with the sounds of airplane engines. He said, "That's a British fighter plane." And he flew by beside the boxcars, dropping red flares all the way. He was flying toward the railroad yard that was ahead of us. They had taken the locomotive away to use it someplace else. We were just dead on that track. We didn't know at the time, but up at the top of this hill, this big building—was a stalag—a place called Limburg. And about half an hour after that plane flew over, British bombers came over there, at a low

47

altitude—bombing. Dropping five-hundred-pound bombs between the train and this wall of dirt (I think it was all rock, anyhow). And we didn't know until later that the train wasn't the target. We thought it was. But some of the bombs hit so close and rocked those cars we thought they were going to upset.

Up the line from our car, there was a little fellow who was able to get his hand out of some rotten wood on the side of the car he was in, and he was able to reach the lock that held the door shut. So he got out, and then came back opening all the doors. The guards—when the air-raid alert went off, left their stations along the train, and went to an air-raid shelter. So they weren't there to stop us. When we got our door opened, we jumped out the door, my buddy and I, and we ran—about fifteen feet—and ran smack into a barbed-wire fence. And the bombs were flying—falling all around us. And I told him, "Let's move back from the train. If that's the target, let's move as far back as we can." So we got up and left, and right where we were standing, a bomb landed and exploded. Fortunately, the explosion went out over our heads. The grace of God again! The target for the British bombers was an oil refinery in the railroad yard ahead of the train in Limburg. Unfortunately, some bombs hit the large building, which was the stalag where we were to be, but the place was full. Many men and officers were killed in that bombing.

Now, after a while, the bombing stopped, and the guards came back, rounded us up, and put us back in the cars again. And the planes all left. I think there were eight men out of some cars killed there. Of course, the Germans had to take care of them. We remained there, and that was the 23rd. And the 24th, of course, the day before Christmas. It was a cold day. The sky was bright with the cumulus clouds all around. It was gorgeous to look up through the cracks in these boards in the car. And the air-raid sirens went off, and after a while, we could look up and see American B-17 bombers flying eight and ten abreast! As high as we could see them! And they were flying—the next ones came eight or ten abreast—flying nose-to-tail! It took two hours for them to pass over. After they passed over for a while—a long time—some German city or some building or factory was really getting peppered. The ground shook, and the rumbling in the distance, you could hear. If you wanted to be hateful, you could say, "Well, you deserve it." And sometimes I guess we felt that way. But anyway, I had a feeling for the people to have this showered down on them and no place to go.

Anyhow, the 25th came around, and nothing happened that day. It was a beautiful day. Snow fell, and some of us sang—in all of our misery—a couple of carols. God was still with us. Not that He was just with us. He's with everybody. But you see the things that happened. What did he want with us? We don't know.

Two days after that, there was a bump in these cars. And the locomotive had backed in and hooked onto us. We discovered that they had to wait those couple of days because the target for those bombers was an oil-refining plant in this railroad yard that was ahead of us—where we backed in from originally. Now they found a locomotive, and we were on our way. We went through Frankfurt, Germany, which was a large rail center. We went through at night, and we could see with a little bit of light that was out there in the yard, because everything was blacked out. But the train went slowly through there, and we could see cars there with tanks on them, being hauled to the front and everywhere. But we kept on going. And finally, after nine days in the cars, with no food, no water, no anything—we arrived at the first stalag. A stalag is a prison camp for prisoners of war. We arrived there in the afternoon, and when we crawled off the cars, we could hardly walk. We were so stiff from being locked in there for all that time, and they tried to double-time us into the camp, which didn't work. They did force us to walk as fast as possible.

This was about half a mile, if I remember, from the rail-head to a field where we stood. Like I say, we arrived there along about three o'clock in the afternoon. I don't know how many of us there were. There were a lot of cars. I didn't get a chance to count them all. But the wind was blowing there, probably forty miles an hour, on this open field. Somebody asked the German how cold it was. He said twenty-below-zero—was the chill factor. Now, we still had our steel helmets. This camp was operated by the British. After we got inside (which took awhile), we discovered that these were prisoners taken at Dunkirk five years before. They had been there long enough that they would not let us go in that camp until we were deloused. They had fixed up a method, and they had an English doctor there. In fact, they had an English preacher there—Church of England. I got to see him later.

We stood out there—I still had my watch. They tried to steal it a couple of times, but I snitched it back before they got away with it, and they couldn't go after me—the Germans. About three o'clock in the morning, we stood out there all that time, and finally, thirty of us went in. They were taking us in thirty at a time. Just before that, they started putting men in an empty warehouse. Well, that was just about as cold as outside, except we didn't have the wind. We stood there, and it was three o'clock the next morning until I got in—along with the other twenty-nine men in that group—and we took our clothes off, and we gave them to them, and we had a shower—a hot shower. I don't know where they got the hot water and all this, but they did. And our clothes came back to us. Most of us didn't have any belongings anymore—all our toilet articles were back where we came from. When we were falling around and doing what we did, you lose what you have in your pockets. I had a little Testament, and I lost it somewhere. And I had a little notebook—lost that after a while, too.

They took us in, and by the time I got in, it was getting to be about six o'clock in the morning, and the British were up, and they said that they were going to share a brew with us. They had a barracks leader, and he said, "The Yanks have come in overnight, and we're going to share what we have. There isn't room enough for all of you who are coming here, but we'll share with you what we have." So they did. They gave us a tea-which was what their brew was—and we stayed there for a couple of days, and they did interrogate us there. And I managed to get my watch in there, and the man took it, but I got it back again a couple of days later. The Germans used to send men to infiltrate the prison camp to find out what people were saying or who was getting ready to try to escape and all of these things, so you had to be careful where you talked.

We stayed there for a couple days, because—oh! And one thing I forgot! When we went in the gate there, they took all of our steel helmets from us. And the army that year had issued combat boots with rough leather on the outside—about six or seven inches high. Some of the guards out there liked those, and they put a pistol in your side and said, "Take your shoes off." And you're standing there in the snow! Fortunately, I missed that—Grace of God again. I still had my boots.

We went down for interrogation, and they interrogated what our organization was, and all we were required to give was our name, rank, and serial number, which we did. After the third day there—in fact, the third day there was my birthday—it was the seventh of January. And I celebrated my twenty-sixth birthday in Stalag 4-B, about sixty miles from Berlin. Nobody to celebrate with me, but I knew it was my birthday. I did get to write a letter to my wife, and you had to be very careful what you wrote, because they censored all of them, and they might not send it at all. But she did get it eventually. She never knew I was captured until I was liberated.

But anyway, they picked out eighteen hundred of us whom they were going to take out of the camp—all non-commissioned officers. They were going to send us to a new camp. So the next day, the train was there, and they said it would be a two-day trip. They gave us our rations for that trip. And our rations were a little piece of meat—more like corned beef, and it looked about the size of a sugar cube, and a couple little biscuits. Now in that camp, those few days while we were there, we only got a little bit of some food portions that had come in for the British. They gave one of the biscuits out of their food parcels, and that's all we had for that little bit of time. So we had these biscuits and that little piece of meat—that was our two-days' ration.

So we got on another train and went; it didn't take two days. They sent us over to the Czechoslovakian border, near a city named Gorlitz. I believe we arrived on or about January 12, 1945. And they left us there. We were the first Americans in this camp. In fact, that camp wasn't even listed on many maps that showed where prison camps were. It was 12A. There were eighteen-hundred of us who went in there. We all went in there, we stayed there for about two weeks in a couple of buildings they had, and then they transferred us over where they had some French prisoners, who moved out, and they put us in their place.

We got what they called—they called it "Skilly." And it

was like a soup—a water soup. Soup made with things like carrot tops or turnip tops, or something like that boiled in it. Or little pieces of rutabaga. Not much of anything. That's what we'd get once a day, and that was all. Once and a while, we'd get a little bit of German army bread, which is a sourdough bread made with potato flour—with sawdust on it. All of us still had diarrhea. There was nothing we could do about it. There was no medical care.

The Serbians and some of the French left the stalag every day to go to town to work. They bribed the guards to let them out and in again. Cigarettes were money in the prison camps and outside—especially American ones. Someone told us that a Luger—a German pistol with ammunition—went for two thousand cigarettes. The Serbians would buy or barter for flour, rice, or white civilian bread, whatever was available and sell it in the stalag. The black market was active. Coffee, tea, white shirts, watches, rings and things with any value could be sold or traded.

One of the Serbians who spoke some English would carefully come into our compound to sell his wares secretly. On one of his visits, I showed him the fairly decent wristwatch, which up to this time I had managed to keep hidden from the Germans. I asked him what he thought he could get for it. He said probably twelve packs of American cigarettes. So I gave him my watch, and in a few days, he brought the cigarettes. We had no place to keep anything, and things got stolen. I divided them with the men from "B" Company, whom I could trust. So now we could buy some of the things the Serbs brought in, and some of my men shared in a taste of a little something more than nothingness that was there. We did smoke some of the cigarettes. In the morning, it seemed that a puff of a cigarette helped to break the hunger pangs. But I knew this would vanish when the cigarettes were gone. Somebody had a little tin box, and as the cigarettes burned down too far to smoke, the man with the box of butts would take a cigarette paper (which was available), roll a cigarette, and pass it around so we all got a puff. Finally this stopped.

With every passing day, I noticed I had to pull my belt a little tighter. There was nothing to do but talk, and even sleeping was difficult. At the end of the barracks we were in, there was a latrine, and it had room for one person. At night if it was occupied and someone needed it, and decided to go outside, he would have been killed, for the guard towers had machine guns aimed down the line of barracks.

One or two things broke the seeming quiet despair—not that it helped us, but it surely made a lot of noise—was the first jet airplane that flew over the stalag about three times a week.

On days when the sun shone even in the cold or in front of the dirty windows, we could find somewhere to sit and around our trousers we could catch the lice that were there between our fingernails and squeeze the blood out of them—probably ours! Depression and despair could be seen in most of us. But God's grace was there, although hunger and emaciation makes it terribly hard to keep things straight.

In that camp, we had an opportunity to go to a Sunday service. There was a place in the camp that had, two buildings coming together on a "V." And it looked like—what was remaining there—as if it at one time had been a place where they had flowers on shelves. So this priest from the Church of England had gone along over there from 4-B, as I recall. Sunday came, and they said, "If you want to go to a Sunday service, they're going to have one over at this place." So there were about six or eight of us who went over there. There had been glass in the windows, but now there was no glass in the windows, and the cold wind was whistling through there. We had Communion that day! And I thought, *My! This is wonderful! We can celebrate the death and Resurrection of our Savior, even though it's not Easter! And in a situation where we don't know whether we're ever going to get out of!* The priest had a message that day, and he had a little bit of tea that he had brought. He had it heated up pretty well. Incidentally, we had been given mess kits at the other camp before we got here. It was like a little pan that you'd put on a stove—like a saucepan—all rusty with a handle on it. And they gave us a rusty spoon, about the size of a tablespoon, That was our mess kit, because most of us had lost ours. And they also gave us a blanket, about thirty inches square, and if you held it up to the light, it looked like a piece of burlap bag. The wind in this area was strong with the cold, where we had our Sunday service, and we had to drink our tea quickly before it froze. The Communion was very meaningful.

29   *Start of Our March*

Now, January had gone, and it was February 1945. The Russians were starting their drive from the east, and we were right in the path of their advance. So on the fourteenth of February—Valentine's Day—we walked out of that camp and started a march that was going to take us over a lot of Germany, and cover somewhere between five and six hundred miles. It was a cold, icy day. It snowed the night before, again. As we were moving out, we saw the people of that area who were going away from their homes in a mass exodus. Everything that they had possessed that had wheels on it, they had loaded their few belongings they were taking with them. They were running away in fear of the Russians. And the highways there were built over rolling hills. You could see from one hill to the other one far ahead. The columns were as long as the eye could reach. We walked past them. Eventually we overcame them and passed beyond them. They were moving slowly. And they moved us along pretty rapidly.

The first city we came to—that we had anything to look at—was the city of Meissen. And I noticed that when we went through there, that there was a very large wooden bridge that bridged a river that passed through the city. It looked as if it had been there for years. If you were there looking for architecture, there was much there to look at, if you were on a tour. We weren't on a tour. But we were on a march through the place where they made Dresden china, which has been so popular for many years. We continued on. We walked country roads. We walked through towns sometimes. Even the Hitler Youth came out when we were walking through. They'd come out, and they'd kick us in the shins. These little six- and seven-year olds—wearing uniforms. They would come up with something like a baseball bat and bat you with it. Or sometimes they'd take us through towns where the Air Force had just passed through a night or two and demolished half the place. The people would spit on us, and they'd throw brick bats at us. And they clubbed us when we went through. There wasn't a thing we could do about it but just try to avoid it until we got out of the place.

Every day we made an average of about twelve miles. Now twelve miles for a well-trained soldier who has been trained to walk and carry his rifle and all of his pack that goes with it—and is fed—is not much to do. But when you're so emaciated that your clothes are beginning to hang on you and your energy is just not there anymore, along with diarrhea, which just saps the life fluids out of your body—it's hard to do. But you do it, or the alternative is to get shot. So you try. And within myself, I made a statement to myself that I was going to try to do this as God gives me strength. That if I die, it will be because I have no longer the capability of living. They're not going to get a chance to shoot me for doing something. I'm going to be as strong as I can. I had a will to live.

Day after day—sometimes we would get put up in barns. They would take a lot of barns that they would commandeer to put us in. In a way, that was good. In a way it wasn't good. Now there are two kinds of ways the Germans took care of prisoners of war. I know their situation—that they could have released us. Of course, they wouldn't do that. But anyway if you're in a prison camp, there's not always any heat in the place. There's no more food sometimes. But you're out of the elements. We were out there—if it rained, we walked, just the same. If it snowed, we walked just the same. We never got dry. We never really got warm. Now sometimes, in a barn at night, to get out of the wind and the blowing rain and the blowing snow was a blessing. In other times, when we got into the barns, the barns was so full of fleas from animals, and we already—most of us had fleas and lice. I had things called scabies—I didn't know what they were until I got back to American control. I think the lice and things had a dance on our abdomens before we went to sleep—and we were dog-tired.

We didn't get to sleep early. And shortly after daylight broke, they came, rolled the barn doors open, and got us out of there. And they came in—if the barn happened to have any hay or straw or anything in it, some of them would crawl into the straw and try to get some warmth from it. And the next morning, they would open the doors so fast, they'd send German soldiers in a hurry with their bayonets and rifles, and they would take it and jab it down through the straw, to see if anybody was hiding there. And there was the possibility of getting the bayonet through you.

So anyhow, I'd like to share with you for just a moment when another man and I—a tech sergeant I met from a chemical mortar company—had been with my company for a while, and I got separated from the column when I fainted one day, and they went on, and there was another column coming, and they took me over with that one. And I missed some of the men of my own company. Well, I met this man, and we hit it off very well. We talked about things, and we were both about the same age. He was from Illinois somewhere, and of course, I was from Pennsylvania. And we talked about many things.

And the subject most of the time was what we shouldn't talk about—what you don't have is what you talk about. We talked about food, and he said how when he was at home the wonderful pies his mother used to make, and then

58

his wife made certain things—and how they made them all of this. We got along, and incidentally, on the road, the food came very erratically. Sometimes—and not every day—they would give us something to drink. And it was called Ersatz (imitation) coffee—substitute coffee. It was made from parched barley. They'd take barley, parch it and brown it, and then they'd put water with it. They'd boil it and make a drink out of it, and it had at least some flavor.

When I was released from the so-called "hospital" where they told me I had pneumonia, there was a stalag nearby that had French soldiers in it. They put about fifteen of us in an empty building to wait two days for an American column. While there, the French "generously" shared an American Red Cross food parcel with the fifteen of us. It was my understanding that a prisoner was to receive one a week. However, we all got a little. I got a little bit of sugar and a little bit of "klim" (dried milk). They gave us their coffee substitute, I added my sugar and klim, and it was rather tasty. However, this was their only generous offer for the two days. The rest of the two days was "Skilly."

On the march, our main food was German army bread—I said before that it was black bread made with potato flour and covered with sawdust. When it was fresh, it tasted the best. And the texture of it was somewhat like gingerbread in the United States—a dark bread. It was tastiest when it was fresh. But it should be held for a day or two until it gets a little age on it, because it makes the diarrhea worse. Frequently—about once every two weeks—not regularly—they would give us our ration of bread. And they'd take that loaf—which was just about ten or twelve inches long, and maybe four inches across—and they'd divide that among twelve men. So you might get a small slice of it, and we had a Stalag disc they gave us, which is a piece of steel with a prisoner number on it, and we used that as our measuring gauge. And somebody who had a pocket knife—or still had one, rather—he would cut this, and we'd watch this very closely that he didn't cut a sixteenth of an inch more for himself than us. But that's what we got for that time. In the beginning, we covered about twelve miles a day. Now we averaged seven.

In the beginning of March—after we had been on the road about two weeks—I woke up one morning—we were in a barn that time—this buddy of mine—we were sharing our field jackets. One of us would put his field jacket on the ground at night for a ground cloth and then put his blanket on top of that, and then the other one would put the blanket on—we'd sleep in the fetal position, back-to-back. We never took our boots off, because they were so hard and cold, we'd never have gotten them back on again. They stayed wet the whole time. Then we'd take the field jacket and spread mine across the top of us, hoping that the heat from each one of our bodies would help us.

Anyway—I started to tell you about what happened one night. I got up in the morning, and if you didn't get out quick, they had dogs that came in—and I'd seen those dogs bite right straight through a man's wrist, and even the handlers never took the muzzle off of them until they fed them. And then they took it off, and they put it right back on again. This barn had the doors that rolled on it, instead of hinged. They opened the door real early in the morning, and they started to throw the dogs in and scream and kick and curse at us to get us up.

I reached over and said, "Come on, Bill, these maniacs are coming in." I shook him, and Bill was stiff as a board. Rigor mortis had set in during the night. I was going to take his dog tag, but they wouldn't let me. They said they'd take care of that.

I had a terrible headache the night he died, when I woke

up. I knew I had a fever, because my head ached, and I was hot. I'd had pneumonia before. I knew what pneumonia was like. I thought, *Well, what am I going to do with this.* But you have to get up and go. And I thought, when my buddy died—I said, "I'll miss you, but I'm sure—" We had talked about all of this along the road—that he was in a better place.

So that day, as every day I walked along, I would pass out. I'd faint. And it seemed like one of the guards was a real tall, young fellow. He had lost an eye on the Russian front. And then they put him over here to guard us. It seemed every time I would pass out, he'd be there when I came around. If I didn't come around, he carried an old Mauser rifle—with bolt action. He'd be kicking me in my left side, because I fell forward on my face. And if I didn't get up quick enough, he'd take the butt of the rifle to me. And when I finally came around and struggled to get up and get dizzy and be unstable for a while, he would holler at me, "ROUSS, ROUSS, ROUSS!" [Move! Get moving!] And I struggled, and I'd go ten feet and pass out again.

One time, we were traveling back on some rural roads, and we met a whole lot more soldiers. And here, they tripled the guard on us. Now our column really stretched out for a long distance. I don't know how many were there. There were 1,800 of us who started originally. But I had switched columns, so I didn't know who I was with.

Regardless, I passed out ten or more times one day. And we had made about ten of the twelve miles, and I struggled along to continue. And there were numerous others who passed out. And they commandeered some farmer's sloping side wagon and his horse, and they helped us to get up on there so they could take us the rest of the way. Now, we stayed that night out in the open, and that was a miserable night.

61

Oh! I was cold! I shivered all night long, and there was no way I could get warm. And in the morning, they said they were going to take some of us to Lazarette. In their words, that's a hospital. So again, they commandeered somebody's old truck. They had trucks and buses over there that burnt carbon monoxide gas. They'd put wood in a tank, heat it, and drive the carbon monoxide off of it, and then burn it in their engines, because they were short of gasoline. This farmer had an old truck that he had one of these tanks on, and they took ten of us over to this so-called hospital. Well, when I went in the door—got off this truck and went in the door, I fainted. It was a building about forty feet square—just an open space. And if you'd have put a bale of hay on there, that would have been more than what was on the floor in there for a bed.

Well, as I entered in the door, I fainted, and a couple of guards picked me up and roughly threw me over against the wall, sitting on the floor. And after a while—after I was there about an hour, there were two men who came in. One was Russian, and his uniform looked like he had just come in from working on his car. It looked like it was greasy, and all like that. Another one there was a man with a pretty blue overcoat on. He wasn't German. Here he was, a Serbian doctor, and I couldn't communicate with him. But there was somebody from up there in the coal regions in Pennsylvania—Slovak or something—he was able to understand him and talk with him. So this doctor (I found out what he was later) had told this man from up in the coal regions that he had been a chief surgeon in a large Serbian hospital before he was captured. He examined me and said that I had pneumonia. He said, "I don't have anything to give you."

Now the International Red Cross had brought medical supplies and stuff in for prisoners of war. But sometimes they got exhausted, and sometimes they got stolen. But he said, "I don't have anything. I have one injection here. It's not for what you have, but I haven't had a chance to use it. I'm going to give it to you." I asked him to tell him, "Why give it to me if it's not going to do me any good?" He said, "I'm going to give it to you, and it won't hurt you." So he gave me the shot in the butt, and then I stayed there until the next day—another column was coming through. And they sent me out with that one. Here again was "One-Eye," this skinny guy who was always there when I fainted—and one day, we saw this new bunch of soldiers up there waiting for us.

Now we were in a place where we were going up a foothill. Walking along a foothill rather than on the rural road—why we were up there, I don't know. Or what was there? They tripled the guard. They put three times as many guards on us as they had before. And up in there, what we were walking on was more like a logging trail than a road. So on the side of the road over—what I called a "berm," dirt and stuff was piled up. And I was having trouble with my swollen right ankle. I had to unbuckle my boot, and I couldn't buckle it. It pained me terribly. And it would go out from under me, as if I only had one leg. And I'd fall over, and one reason I fell from fainting, and the other, my right leg went out from under me. And it pained like somebody sticking a knife in it. The more I walked, the more it hurt, but still I had to go.

That day, this pile of dirt I was walking on to try to keep out of a whole bunch of mud at the side, so I wouldn't slip and fall in it. And I slipped on this, because my leg wasn't holding me, and I fell down, and he came over and gave me a kick to get up. And I struggled to get up—it was terribly painful. He told me to go! Well, about the time I turned to go, I fainted. And when I came to, this happened five times.

Now, at the end of our column, and the column passed on beyond me—they passed, and I couldn't keep up with them then. So the end of the column was coming, and I didn't know that at the end of the column there was a German sergeant walking there and a British doctor. The British doctor could speak the German—I guess he was one who was captured at Dunkirk, but he happened to get onto this column. Now he had no medical supplies or anything—somebody told me all of this later. After about the fifth time I fell, this "one eye" (I called him)—he took his rifle, pulled the bolt back, and he put a bullet in the chamber. And I was standing there, trying to stand and not fall. And he has this up—putting it up to his shoulder—about six inches in front of my face, and he's about ready to shoot me, when this German sergeant and this British doctor came around a bend in this logging road.

The German sergeant hollered at him, and he stopped. He took his rifle down and took the round out of the chamber. The sergeant said something to him, I don't know what. The British doctor came over and said to me, "Are you having a lot of problems?" "Yessir." He asked, "What's your problem?"

I said, "Well, I'm fainting. I'm so weak I can't keep moving." And I told him about this thing in my leg.

"Oh, my!" he said. "I don't know what to do for you. I don't have anything. I can't do anything. We'll have to keep going."

I would drag along for a while, then I fainted time after time, and sometimes (there were many of us like that) they'd get somebody with a wagon or something to pick us up and move us up in the column farther, and we'd get down and have to lie there in the snow or whatever until we finally got energy to go on. It went on like that—finally the weather started to get a little bit better. We were then—over most of March—and I still had the headache, and I still had the fever and everything.

A long about the middle of April, it started to get a little bit better. And I'd say it was, April 23rd or something like that, when we moved into a town—a small town. We only stayed there part of a day. Then we walked about three miles to another town—a little bit larger town.

Spring was starting to move in, and in that town, there was a guest house. Most towns had guest houses in them, and this one had a barn behind it, which most of them had. And some of us—most of us—were called the "krank"—the sickest—a man I knew had a leg muscle that had a chunk shot out of it—the blood was frozen on his leg. I say it was the Grace of God that pulled us through when it was cold and we felt like our next step would be our last. And it was the Grace of God that it was winter, because the cold slowed their bleeding. And God was there. And some who had various things wrong with them that had never been treated, and they survived.

As time wore on, it was May 10, and as the weather warmed, our spirits improved, and occasionally we got war news that our ordeal may be ending. God's grace was still working. Now on that day, the guards kind of eased up a little bit. Before we got into that town, we passed a couple of road intersections, and you could see where somebody had dug some entrenchments where they could put a machine gun there to aim it down the road if somebody would come in. There was nobody in those holes when we came by. We came into this town, and the worst of us—the ones who were the least able to walk or who had untreated wounds—they put in the guesthouse part. They had a large room there. I guess there might have been two-hundred of us in there. So anyway, they left us in there in the daytime.

And at night, they made us go back and stay in the barn. They wouldn't let us in there overnight.

On the eleventh of May, they let us go out to a little stream in back of the barn. And they let us go out there and put our hands in the water. I hadn't touched water that whole time—hadn't washed my hands. It felt so good to get some water on my hands. The sun started to come up that day, and it was bright. Early that morning, British Spitfire fighters came flying over the town as all six machine guns rattled away. There were a few shots possibly from one of those fortifications we saw on the way in could have been their target. But they made several sorties over the town, and the guards made us go in when those planes went over—the air raid alert sounded, and we went back into the barn.

The next morning—the twelfth of May, I was still sick. I was in the barn. About 6:30 in the morning, an American Army captain walked in along the guest house back to the barn where we were all staying—at least part of that group was. He said, "Hey, men—go out and take this town!" He said, "We heard you were over here. I was not supposed to come over this way, but I wanted to come over and give you the town." And he said, "If you want to go get a bed to sleep in, go in a house, and if they resist you, throw them both out of their bed and out the house. We are conquerors. Take whatever food they may have." I'm sure he meant what he said, but I'm not sure he was aware of our weak and emaciated conditions. However, he and the two men with him were gifts from God!

FREEDOM!

30 Trip to Air Field at Hildesheim Hospital Stay

I walked over and asked him, "Captain, suppose the Germans counterattack and come back gather us up again?" "Well," he told me, "before I arrived here, I called back and asked for front-line military police to come and pick up the guards you have and take them away." And he said, "We understood that you have some who are wounded and some who need medical care. I've called the medics, and they are sending ambulances up to pick up the worst of the sick and injured."

When I asked him about the counterattack, he said, "Well, you'll be traveling up the road where we are standing, and about three or four miles out of town, as you travel that road, you'll see more tanks than you've ever imagined existed." And he said, "Now don't worry. There's a lot of back-up. But I must go." So he said, "Make yourselves at home."

It didn't take long to clean out the bakery up the street. The old baker objected to it, because we didn't have any coupons for it, but we cleaned it out in short order. And we didn't need that rich food with all that sugar and stuff. We even got hold of some butter and raw milk, which we didn't need. Our diarrhea was bad enough without adding to it. However, that day, I walked in on the porch of the farmer's house, by his kitchen. He had the door open, because it was a beautiful May day. It happened to be the twelfth of April. And I heard his radio, and it had an announcement on it from the BBC—the British Broadcasting Company. He announced sadly that President Roosevelt had died that day in the United States.

So we stayed there about three or four more days, and we found enough food around to satisfy us. We couldn't eat much anyway. And after three or four days—whatever it was—I've forgotten—they came with what I call cattle trailers, and they could haul a lot of men in there. And they came—a convoy of them—picked us up and started on the road back to American control.

As the captain had told us, about four miles out of town, lined up on both sides of the roads, were American tanks. The tankers were working on their vehicles or washing their clothes—washing the oil out of them—with some gasoline, I guess. They were part of Patton's army, and they had run out of gas.

Now we traveled sixty miles, and there were many miles where we passed tanks. The convoy stopped at one place, and right beside one of these tanks, I was standing close to the outside of the trailer. And I said, "Hey, Sarge [or whoever he was]! What kind of tank is that?"

"What do you mean, what kind of tank is that?"

"We never saw one of those."

He asked, "Who are you guys?"

I said, "We're prisoners of war that they just liberated."

"Really?!" he said. "Why, it's a General Grant."

"Well," I said, "the last that we saw were Shermans."

"Well," he said, "this is new in this year, and it's dandy!" He said "Wait a minute!" So he goes and tells his buddy, and they start throwing us those chocolate bars that the army had that don't melt very easily. We didn't need chocolate, but we ate it. And we thanked him for it and went on.

And finally we arrived at a captured air field. Now what was going on there—the Air Force was flying C-47s, and the shuttle trip was from that airfield to LeHavre—at the gasoline dump. They were hauling five-gallon cans filled with gasoline, and unloading the cans of gas. And they were taking POWs back to the LeHavre—to a place where we would go back into American control again. So there were a lot of men there. We had a precursory physical—the doctors there did check our blood pressure, and they poured DDT over our heads, because we were lousy. And they assigned us all a number and a group that we would be with. If I remember correctly, each one of those C-47s, when they went back to LeHavre, and even with ten or twelve of us they took along. And there were lots of them flying. They wanted to get a lot of gasoline up there for Patton.

And the Red cross trucks were there—we could go down and get coffee and donuts. We didn't need donuts, either. However, they had other food there, and we didn't get like you'd go to a fancy restaurant, because the men were coming and going so rapidly. But the next day, they called out the group we were in. I picked up some of my men back there. And we got on the C-47, and the war wasn't quite over yet. They said there were still a few stragglers—German fighter planes around. We stayed down to treetop height over the mountains and made it safely back to the airfield at LeHavre. They unloaded us, they promptly taxied the plane over, and they were loading it for another trip back to the airfield.

In the meantime, we went over and got on a French train, and we traveled relatively short distance. Then we got off the train, and we went to—I forget where they took us by trucks or whether we walked, because it wasn't far from the railhead where we got off to a camp called "Lucky Strike." Now this was a place all set up by the army that had pyramidal tents—the square tents with the pointed center. And in

71

there, there were cots—well, it was still a little cool. They had blankets on them. And we got there, and we started our processing. We had a chance to get a hot meal. We couldn't eat very much. Our stomachs had shrunken to the point that a little piece of something was almost too much. However, they said to eat as much as we think we could handle.

Then they took us over to a building. And we went in there, took our clothes off, emptied our pockets if we had anything, because they said, "You're not going to get them back."As we took our clothes off, we threw them in a pile, and they picked them up right away. And then we got showers, and we got toilet articles. I got something that I could shave with. I got a toothbrush and a couple of small face towels and soap. My! It was nice to get in that hot water and feel like a person again! All new uniforms they gave us. We had a rank—they gave us our chevrons and said we could put them on so that they could identify us. We also went to a new information place, where they wanted to know our name, our rank, our serial number, and what our organization was, and where our family was, and who to send a telegram to.

So my wife told me later that she never knew where I was from December on. I was just listed as "Missing in Action." Then she found us (the same as many other new mothers), and they paid all of us twenty dollars, there at Lucky Strike. They had some souvenirs you could buy. The problem was that they didn't know how much back pay we had coming. They didn't know how many months we were incarcerated.

In the meantime, we were free to go over to a place where you stood up to eat, because there were so many men coming in and out. They had French cooks there, and they made cookies! We were free to have that, and they had egg nog there, and we could come and drink that any time we wanted. Unfortunately, there was one man who got carried away with the cookies. He ate so many of them that it killed him. And our stomachs couldn't take much.

However, when we got there, I still had my pneumonia. I still had my terrible headache and ached all over. And I knew that I still had a fever. But when we got there, they said there was a three-day processing that would be taking place. The first day would be what they did—took the information, gave us showers and stuff, and we were free to go and lie down on our cot in the tent anytime during the day if we got tired. We were free to go back and get something to eat, or egg nog—that was supposed to be rich for our stomachs. And other things they had processing with, some people got physical help, because they had doctors there—well, they had a number of them. And they went to the medics, and they took care of some of the things—their wounds, they dressed. But I held off. I put up with what I had for those months, and finally, late on the evening of the second day, I had been through my processing, and if you were through your processing on the third day, and if there was a transport ship in the harbor at LeHavre, you got to go home on that ship.

So anyway, I went to the medics, and I thought, *Oh, there'll be a corporal-a T-5 in there (Charge of Quarters)*. I went in, and he asked, "Can I help you, Sarge?" I said, "Yeah. How about getting some of the APC pills? I have a headache." He said, "Well, we can take care of that."

But I didn't know that there was a doctor in back of the tent fly there at his desk. He opened that up, and he came out, and he asked, "What's your problem, Sarge?" I said, "Well, I have a headache, Doctor." He said, "How long have you had it?" I said, "Oh, a couple of months." He said, "Why don't you hop up on that examining table there, and let me check your heart out." He said, "We'll get your temperature." I said, "Oh, Captain, I don't have a temperature." He said, "Well, let's check it anyway."

Of course, he had the authority, and he checked it, and he asked, "How long did you tell me you had this?"

"Well," I said, "It's strange—I can tell you the very day. It started on the first of March." He said, "You've had this all that time?" And I said, "Well, there was nobody to treat me." And I told him about the swelling in my right ankle.

He said, "Well, that will go away as you get better food." But he asked, "What tent are you in?" They were all numbered, and they had the cots numbered in there. We had good army blankets that would keep us warm in the cool evenings. He said to me, "Well, what cot?" I told him. He said, "What do you have there?"

"Well, the only thing I have is a couple towels they gave us and toilet articles, and such as that." He said, "Well, just sit down and wait." I said, "Okay. What do you want me to do?" He said, "Sit down and wait. I'm going to send an ambulance driver down and get your things and bring them up here."

"Oh?"

"Yes," he said, "we have a field hospital here. And you're going to it tonight! If I send you down for it, you won't come back. I'm not going to let you go home as sick as you are." He asked, "How many days of your processing do you have in?"

I said, "Well, this is the second."

"Uh, huh," and he said, "there's a ship in the port, too. At this time, if they don't know any different, they probably have your name on a list to board that ship tomorrow."

I said, "Well, I sort of hoped that, and I wanted to get rid of this headache so I wouldn't take it along home."

He said, "Yeah, you were going to try to sneak by me and go home as sick as you are!" And he said, "Sergeant, you dare not go home as sick as you are. You have people waiting there?"

I said, "Yes. I want to see my wife and my young son."

He said, "Well, they can wait a few more days so that you can go home fit and rid of what you have!"

So they put me in the hospital, and I went over there probably 8:00 that night. And a big tent—those field hospitals. They had cots in there, and I went in, a nurse met me, and she told me where I could put my articles. She said, "They'll probably assign you to another bed, but you can just put them there for now. The doctor will be here in just a couple of minutes."

So the captain came in—the doctor of medical corps. He told her, "Nurse, I'd like to have him moved down close to that heater there." (The evenings got cool.) And he said, "I want you to get a curtain and put up around him. I want him to strip completely." He sat me down, I looked at him, and he said, "I can see scabies around your neck and stuff." So he said, "I'd like to examine him all over." So he did, and he gave me a very thorough examination. After a while, he looked at my scabies, and he said, "Oh, my! You've got scabies from your chin to your ankles." He asked, "Doesn't it itch?"

I said, "Yes! Terribly!" So I said, "By the way, Doctor, you're the second doctor who has told me that I had scabies." I asked him, "Doctor, what are scabies?"

"Well," he said, "you know what chiggers are?" I said, "Yes, I know what chiggers are. They bore down in your skin."

The doctor said, "These scabies are little mites that live in dirt and filth. They get on you, and they bore down into your skin. They lay their eggs after they're down there. And they have a serum that comes with these eggs. When you scratch them as they itch, you just carry these eggs to a new

75

spot, and they hatch, once again, and burrow down under your skin. It progresses all around, because you just help spread it when you scratch. Of course, you don't know that."

"Well," I said, "I'll be glad to get rid of them. By the way, how long will it take to get rid of these?"

He said, "Well, tomorrow morning, you will not itch anymore."

I said, "That quick?"

"Yes," he said, "That quick. I'm going to give your nurse a prescription to get a salve from the pharmacy. I want you to rub it all over your body as much as you can reach. We'll have an orderly come in here in this curtain with you, and he'll get the ones that are on your back."

I said, "Do I have them there?"

He said, "Yes, you do. I want you to rub this every half hour. Now, you're going to be busy all night. After you rub this all over every spot where you see that there might be one, when you're done, we're going to have water and soap here for you and the man who's helping you, and we want you to wash your hands thoroughly. This salve is deadly poison. It kills the scabies, and it's not injurious to your skin, because it's not going to be on very long. Tomorrow morning you can get a shower. It'll take it that long to work. But the scabies will be dead, and eventually, if they're in your skin, they'll come out. But you won't itch anymore."

And he was true to his word! We were busy all night, and I didn't get ten minutes of sleep, but by the time morning came, I was starting to relax from all this itching and the other things that we had already had showers for, but this got rid of the scabies. The nurse brought my breakfast over, and she asked, "Sergeant, do you want your breakfast?"

I said, "To tell you the truth, Nurse, I am so tired that I

could just flop right down here on the floor and go to sleep, I believe."

"Well," she said, "I don't want you to do that. If you want to sleep . . ."

I said, "Let me ask you something. Do you know of anything they might be planning to do to me for the next four hours?"

She said, "As a matter of fact, you have some medication that you're to have, but we can wake you to give you that. You can sleep all day, if you want to."

"OH!" I said, "that's great! I will eat my breakfast." So I ate as much as I could—as much as my stomach would hold. And I laid down, and the nurse at noontime came—she brought my lunch, and she brought some medication. And she said, "I didn't know whether I could get you awake or not! You were in such a deep sleep!"

I said, "Well I'm really worn out."

She said, "I'm sure you are. Don't like to disturb you, but try to eat a little bit."

So I did, and I went back to sleep, and I didn't wake up until 7:00 that night. And that night, then, even with all that sleep that day, I got the best rest I had in the last six months. They treated me there for my—of course, my head-ache—they fixed that, and they were working on the pneumonia. I was feeling better through that—I wasn't shivering in bed anymore. I rested and did all the things to take care of that. Then they said, "There's no ship in right now, but we expect one in a few days."

So anyway, I stayed there, and while I was lying in the cot, I could hear a diesel engine running, and I figured, "Well, this is their power unit that furnishes power for the hospital." And usually they had two of them—a stand-by one. Both the same capacity, because they needed it for surgery and all the things around the hospital. So I heard these things running, and I was a diesel mechanic. I thought to myself, *Gee, that sounds like a Cummins Diesel.* They have a special sound like most of them do.

A couple of days later, the weather was getting nicer. It was getting later in May, and I guess I went in there—I'm not sure—it might've been the eighth, or something like that. I said to the nurse who was on the daytime, a couple of days later, "Can I go out and walk around outside?" She said, "Sure! The sun's nice out there. Yes!"

I walked over to where I heard this sound of this engine. There were two men there—two soldiers, and they were having a problem. I had heard them trying to start them, and they cranked them, and it sounded like their starters were slowing down, because the batteries were getting weaker. So I walked over, and they said hello. I said, "Hi, men! I see you're having a little problem."

"Yes! We are!"

I said, "What happened that you can't get started?"

"Well," he said, "we changed the oil in the engine that we're not trying to start right now. We changed the fuel filter in this one, and we can't get the fuel system primed. We can't get the fuel up to the injectors." In that engine, you have to pump the fuel up to the injector before you start cranking.

I said, "We can have one engine running in about five minutes. It'd better be, because all your batteries are going to be dead."

"Yeah. We know that," he said. "Pretty soon the hour is coming when they begin some of their surgeries here, and they need the lights and stuff for the surgery."

"Well," I said, "you don't know me at all, but I do know something about these engines. I'll show you how to prime those fuel filters, and you'll know how to do it."

"Ah," he said. "We've got a book, but we never get time to read it."

"That's all right!" I said, "I'll show you."

So I told him what to do to get the fuel up to the injectors. I asked, "Now do you have a box wrench about eighteen inches long?"

"Yeah!" he said.

I said, "Well, you get it, and put it over that handle sticking up there in back of that fan—between the fan and the engine."

He said, "Yeah! What is that?"

I said, "That's the compression release lever. I want you to put that wrench down over there so you don't get your hand in close to that big fan. I want you to pull down on that wrench so that you pull that lever over towards you to hold the valves open to lower the compression so it turns over easier with your low batteries."

"Oh!"

So I said, "Then, we'll take your starter, we'll roll the engine over a little bit, and we'll get it some inertia." And I told the other man, "You go over to that throttle. Whenever I tell you, you pull it wide open."

So we got the engine rolling, and I told him, "You pull the throttle open." And I told the other guy, "Now, let the handle to that lever go back where it was, and let's just see if we're not running."

He pulled the throttle wide open, got a couple of cylinders fired, and then a couple fired, and a couple more fired, and pretty soon the engine was going up to full speed. I'm not bragging about this. This is one of those things that we did many, many times to start those engines.

And one of the guys jumped in a jeep and left. And I asked, "Where'd he go?"

He said, "I don't know! They're running! We can charge our batteries, too."

I said, "Yes."

So, I was talking with the other man, asking where he was from, and pretty soon the other man came back and had a colonel with him. And he told me who the colonel was. He said, "This is Colonel [So-and-So]. He's the commander of this—Chief Medical Officer—Commander of the Hospital." He said, "Are you the man who helped them to get started?"

"Yes."

He asked, "Are you one of the POWs?"

I said, "Yessir, I am."

He asked, "Well, are you through processing?"

I said, "Yes, two days through. Then I came over here. I understand there's a ship in a day or two."

He said, "Yes, there is. Would you like to change your mind and stay here? I will give you a big promotion."

I told the hospital commander that under other circumstances, his offer of a promotion would be very tempting. However, I had a wife and twenty-three-month-old son that I would like to go home to. So he said, "That's a good reason, Sergeant. You go home and enjoy your family." (I did tell the colonel that my MOS was "Diesel Mechanic," and helping those men was the only opportunity to use my knowledge in my Army service.)

So we did sail out of LeHavre, and it took us some days to get across the Atlantic. And we reached New York Harbor, and the fire boats there turned their hoses up in the air. They blew their whistles, and people came out and waved to us and everything. And finally we docked there, got off the ship, and got onto a train that took us to Camp Kilmer. We spent the night there, and the next day, they put us back on the train again and sent us over to Fort Dix, New Jersey, where we received our summer uniforms, which now could be worn. And we stayed there a couple of days, and they also gave us orders. I lacked two points of getting out with the first group that was discharged from the service to go to be separated from the Army, or whatever.

They sent me from Fort Dix to my home, and then I had sixty-three days delay en route to get to Atlantic City, New Jersey. I was allowed to take my wife along. We stayed there, we went in one of the large hotels the Army had taken over. (Unfortunately, it rained every day.) There we were debriefed and got other physical examinations. And we also were reassigned, since I had two points that I had to be before I could be discharged. I was assigned to Indiantown Gap, Pennsylvania, which was a separation point. And when I arrived there, they made me the motor pool dispatcher. There were one hundred trucks that had to go out every morning. They would go down to the railhead at Lickdale and pick up the incoming soldiers to be separated from the service and go home.

Time passed very quickly, and I soon made the two points I was lacking. My time to be separated came, and I thought it would take place there at Indiantown Gap since it was a separation center. But no such thing! About six or eight of us were sent to Phoenixville Hospital, and we were discharged from there. However, I did eventually get home. And as near as some of us can figure, our walk—our forced march with the Germans—was somewhere around 550 miles. We traveled probably close to six-to-eight miles a day on average. Our time on the road on the forced march was eighty-seven days. And we were Prisoners of War for 135 days. Much less than many men suffered, and my heart goes out to them. For many suffered more than I did. I thank You, God, for Your grace that You brought me home, although I didn't know why You wanted me.

Now our total incarceration was 135 days. And 87 days

81

were on the forced march. I had entered the service on the second of July 1942, and I was discharged on October 27, 1945.

31 *Physical, Spiritual, and Mental Effects of POW*

In the earlier parts of my story, I had told you of the events of how we prepared to go to Europe and how we met the enemy later on, and when they had us surrender.

I felt when I went into the combat area that one of several things could happen to me. I am sure any person will wonder what might happen or could happen. I wasn't really afraid to die, although nobody looks forward to it. I was concerned whether I would be crippled or many, many things that could have happened. But as we go further down, I want to share some of the feelings—the frustrations—the spiritual relationship in all of this. And the mental memories have been carried all through these fifty-eight years.

I knew that the enemy probably had people who enjoyed war. Certainly down through the centuries, there have been people who did—people who have conquered someone else to control them. But when I first ordered my men in that position, after we left our work and went up the hill to meet the enemy on that December 16 morning, we had no ammunition. I remembered a saying that I heard from General Bedford Forrest of the Confederate Army in the Civil War. He said—as I've heard it—"He wins who gets there firstest with the mostest." And I felt that day that we were the leastest.

And the frustration that went with it came as I was really angry! We had moved into this area quickly, and the army had put us in this position. I realized that I was a soldier, forced to do what the army said—to obey orders. But the feelings that day of anger and even up till this time now, my heart beats a couple of extra beats at remembering it. It just does not want to go away, just as many other things that I saw and experienced just don't go away.

32　God's Grace in Action

However, we did surrender, and I often wondered—I've struggled with this. I've often wondered about that German major who pulled me out of the river, if the shoe had been on the other foot, would I have done the same thing? Certainly, he was the enemy, and I was the enemy, would I have saved him as part of the enemy? And he had compassion on us. By His grace, God was there that day and spoke to that man. Or he could have been an angel whom God sent to share God's grace with those men who were there with me and our company commander. He gave us the opportunity to live by doing that.

But the time that came after that is another story! I told you that we started to walk, and we did walk an accumulation of three days—as I recall—till we got to a town they called Gerolstein. And I revealed how we got in the boxcars the next day, and we were in there for nine days. One thing that you learn very soon in most cases, when you become a prisoner of an enemy: you're not going to get a lot of food. Most of the time, the nations that do make war concentrate all their means and all their efforts and their natural resources and things—and we're way down the line. Their care for us is not much—at least as I experienced it.

(Interesting sideline: When I got home, my aunt asked me if some of the German people brought us cookies and goodies on the holidays. She said a group of Americans did that for German prisoners who got paid for working at the New Cumberland Army Depot and slept in the same barracks our army used. I understand that many didn't want to go home, and some returned and became citizens. What a contrast from what happened to us!)

Now, I'm not the only POW. There are thousands of us. And many have experienced—many men whom I knew before I went into the service were in the Japanese camps, and they suffered terribly. The Death March and all that which I had heard about. So anyhow, as they transported us to another place, the first stalag we were in—we were only there a short time. And some of the things that go through your mind . . . but God was there that day—that night before Christmas, when the British bombed alongside of our boxcars, we thought they were going to roll over. And I, in my own mind, thought, *What a way to go! Like rats in a trap!* Fortunately, the cars rocked but didn't upset. And as you think back over things, you find that there were blessings there that you didn't realize.

So anyway, the days went on, and the food didn't get any better. We were living on our bodies. I suppose that those of us who were in the same boxcar that I was had the same problems that I had, because if we had food, we all ate what was given to us—it came from the same source. We all had diarrhea, and that just washes the fluids out of your body, and washes the strength away, as anybody who has ever had it knows. And the weakness was becoming greater. When we got off those boxcars, we went to a camp, and then we went to another one, and I related to you in an earlier chapter how on Valentine's Day we started to walk away from the Russians as they drove from the east.

Now, fear is one of the things that I discovered there. Not that it is something that we can do anything about. That's the problem: it's helplessness. You cannot help yourself. If I could have, I would have not been on that train with the cars. If I had the opportunity, I probably would have run away. Unfortunately, you can't do this when somebody's there guarding you. You are at their mercy, and you have to do as they say. Go when they say "Go," and stop when they say "Stop." And you are totally under their control. I know that somebody would say, "Well, it's like being in jail." Well, yes. But in jail, they do feed the inmates. They take care for their health. So this is a totally different situation. My real fear was that someone would get into an argument or "tiff" with a trigger-happy guard, and they would start shooting or turn their ferocious dogs on us.

The winter wasn't over. This was just December. And it soon was January, and we were in another stalag. Now this one was much larger than the one we had been in, and there I wondered, as every day went by, and as the food got less—even though they brought something in that maybe had some rutabaga, which doesn't have much nourishment, or carrot-tops—something like that or turnip tops cooked in water. But it's hardly nourishing. How long could we last as each day we could feel that we were deteriorating?

Then we walked out of there, and went out to walk in the elements—rain, snow, and every day we traveled an average of about eight miles. There was no way of stopping unless you wanted to get shot or try to run away—there were certainly enough guards to stop you, and they would have shot you. The pain of the hunger was awful. I never realized how painful it is to be so terribly hungry that your body just craves for food, and there's nothing you can do about it. That's a feeling that I never realized. Because I never was that hungry. I saw times during the Depression when there were few big meals, but usually there was something you could at least live on.

The mental condition gets confused and weak. When I was a young boy at the church on Sunday evenings, they had a thing for youth. And I learned many Bible verses, and of course, I was active in my local church, where we worshiped. And I tried to recall the verses that would help in my circumstances. In fact, I had aspired to be a minister, but it just wasn't to be at that time. I wasn't looking to be exempted from the draft. I had a definite call that my wife and I had discussed at great length. But as I walked along, I sometimes wondered if I could take the next step. Or sometimes if we had to stand around in a field all night—like a herd of animals, whether the snow came down, or whether it rained and we were getting soaked and the temperature dropped, and we were cold and terribly stiff! Terribly cold!

The Germans had given us blankets? The one I had—I would say it was about three feet square, and I held it up to the light, and it looked like a burlap bag. Most of us had lost our mess kit somewhere. When we went out to meet the Germans, we were told from our division headquarters that we were to be deployed to help stem a little breakthrough! We didn't know at that time the magnitude of this—that there were many divisions and armies—both American and German—that were in a battle that spread over many miles. There was a deadly cost to both sides.

However, there were times, when like I say, we stood all night—and standing all night in the cold—your legs and joints begin to ache. And then when the time comes in the morning when you start to move on, when the guards start to gather everyone on the road, that I didn't know whether I could take another step. They were so stiff and so cold. But somehow or other, I made the step, as did many others. And I—in my own mind early on in the march—I decided that I was going to put every bit of energy into this march wherever it goes. I was going to stay through this—the only way they could get rid of me—they'd have to shoot me or something, or disease would have to take me, because I was going to discipline myself, and I had to go on. And I discovered that when you're very much emaciated and when you're hungry and you're cold or in terrible heat, your mind does not work like it should. The Bible verses that would be encouraging don't come to you as easily, because the mind, also, is not being fed. But I made it, and that determination given by God's grace and my faith, I was going to do everything that I needed to do—that I did not want to give up anymore.

Thoughts and Scripture sometimes come to us—there were many I had learned, and one of them that I couldn't place in the Bible at the time—when Christ said, "Lo, I am with you, even to the end of the world." Or, another way, ". . . even to the end of the age." And so there was no way we could do anything to any guards who kicked us or punched us or took our boots—because that would just stir up a—would break us right there—so it required discipline. I believe that life requires discipline, and there are many things that get in our way—the many troubles we have. But we need to realize that Christ suffered through many things that He never spoke about. Now I don't say that I'm Christ. I'm saying the principle of asking God to help us in all things is important, for He controls all things.

We were totally under their physical control. And I wondered, too, as I was there, I had a wife and a son at home. Would I ever see them again? We had traveled a long way! We wondered frequently how long could we walk? Are they going to walk us till we fall flat on our faces? There was nothing outside to talk about—no news to know what was going on in the world. It seemed very wild. We met a man from the Army Air Corps who had been shot down, and he had some parts, found some wires and other parts, and made a little radio. Because it was forbidden, we had to keep it secret. We passed the word around sometimes that

Patton had gone so far, or other things were happening. But it was just very skimpy.

Loneliness—it's like being alone in a trap. The camaraderie that we had with our friends—yes, we could talk. We talked frequently about food that our mothers made or some Danish or pie or something like that. And it didn't do any good, because it made the hunger just a little bit stronger.

Pain—we were all suffering from the same things: diarrhea, weakness, depression, hunger, and helplessness. We could talk to try to get our minds off the subject—or our minds off the situation. I tried to think of another Scripture that Christ gave. One I remembered particularly was just like Christ made when he was with His disciples and the room was closed—the night of the Resurrection. They were afraid for their lives. And Christ said to them, "Let not your heart be troubled. Believe in God, believe also in me." I tried to believe. I tried to think, "Is this another experience that I must endure, Lord? Will this help me if I ever get to be a minister and share your Word? To try to share it with others?" I thought, *Well, this may be part of the training.*

And there were times when I forgot about Him and went my own way. I felt that He was always there. I recall many times that I was walking, I felt "I am unworthy." Like Paul said, "All of us have sinned and come short of the glory of God." But He always reached out, and sometimes when one of our number would pass away, I felt Him again—that God had taken him to the bosom of His heart.

If we had food and were in good shape—the way we were when we made our many training marches—twenty-five miles, fifty miles—gotten the food that we had, and wouldn't have been under guard on both sides of the road or traveling safety, it might have been an interesting trip. Germany is a very old country, and it has some beautiful places. As a major in the German army said to me about—when he asked me where I was from, and I told him Pennsylvania, and he said, "Oh! It's very much like Germany." And I said, "It truly is. Pennsylvania is a beautiful state." Germany is a beautiful country. It has lakes, and it has rivers, and mountains, and it's just a beautiful place, with forests that are rich, and it's rich with various elements. It was rich with coal, steel ships, and trains that were hauling cargo and things to support the war effort during wartime over there.

Also, when we would come down with some disease because of the lack of medical care, we buried some there in some fields that are unmarked. Not that that would be terrible. But you know, you think about your family at home, and all that goes with it. And the longer we went, the more emaciated we became. Some were down almost like a skeleton. I don't know what I looked like. I know that my clothes were hanging on me. I had to tighten my belt all the time—I was losing my trousers.

I told you earlier that I had a little Testament. Somewhere or another, it's lying in the mud of Germany. It fell out of my pocket. It was gone. I had a notebook. I lost that. Of course, I had nothing to write with anymore. But again, God was always there. Somebody said to me, when they asked me about my experiences—I had shared some of these things, but as I get older, some of them just crop up like they were seeds planted there fifty years ago, and now they're beginning to come forth in my memory.

Why, today, I'm eighty-three years old, and I frequently leave the house to go somewhere, and I tell my wife that I'm going by the grocery store if there's anything she needs before I come home. If I don't write three things down that she wants or whatever, I'll surely forget it. And of course, sometimes my handwriting has become so terrible, and I might not be able to read it. But I'm amazed that—people have told me this—and I'm sharing it with you, that our long-range memories sometimes become much sharper than they had been. Things that happened many years ago—and this experience I'm sharing with you because it happened fifty-eight years ago.

I felt, day-after-day, that sometimes God tries us. Sometimes I wonder, and I've been amazed as I've visited people in the hospitals so many times after I did become a pastor—how much our body is able to sustain—how much it continues to live in spite of what seems would be impossible when things get so bad.

Someone had said to me, "Do you ever think that someone, if they were cagey, could find someplace to hide and escape and just stay there until they die?" I said, "Well, the Germans were pretty thorough in keeping a count of people—of men. And there was no roll call, but periodically there was a head count. They would come back in the line . . ." I said, "I don't know if anybody did that or not."

Or if somebody thought about suicide, I thought about that and things after the war, the conditions that took place. Some of these things brought back some of the problems I had when I was on the road or at a stalag the short time we were there. This is part of the discipline I put on myself: I will not try to take my life. Because it would not accomplish anything. And it wasn't mine to take. If I had been shot or killed, it could have come from another source, but I would not have done it, even though there were times when I considered it. God brought me out of many situations that were too numerous to number. But I had this experience, and I wanted to share it, if you are willing to read this, my rambling.

Well, anyway, before we got into American control, I caught up with some of the men from my original company.

When they put me in a so-called German hospital for a couple of days, and I passed out. I was separated from them and put with another column because there were numerous columns passing back and forth through Germany. As I said, it was a beautiful country. Someone told me at one time—because we had no idea of geography, that we were not too far from Switzerland. And of course, Switzerland is a beautiful nation—also neutral—and if we could have gotten over there, we would have been held there until the war was over. But there again, the Germans were not going to surrender us to them.

So we continued until we were liberated. Now, early on, we started the long march. And after we had surrendered, I felt the frustration come again, and I wondered many times and thought, *Maybe we didn't even do our duty for our nation.* We originally did what we could and what we had to do with. There have been men from other theaters of the war, and other arms of our military and other forces that have said to me, "Well, why did you surrender?" I said, "Well, when you can't do anymore, you have no other thing to do. You're done, and you're at their mercy. If they want to shoot you—" I would have tried to get away somewhere if it was possible; that opportunity never came. But God's grace helped me, and my faith furnished the next step.

People ask me, "Did you ever consider escaping?" Well, yes. I did. But there were a lot of considerations before taking that step. Now I know, in some years back, there was a television program called "Stalag 17." Well, that was not all true to the facts. That was just a movie thing. That's not typical. However, to talk about escaping—before we left these United States, we had an orientation lecture about the enemy and what we would do if we were captured. There is a considerable amount of work that needed to be done to escape. They gave us—while we were there—the marks of rank of German soldiers for an identification. They described what the officers and NCO's wore to identify them and their rank, just as our officers and NCO's have symbols of their rank.

Then one man came on, and he said, "Now, we'll talk about escaping. You're expected to try to escape." Well, that was an order. But he said, "What has to be done—this has to be organized. It has to be planned. You're in a camp, and if you think you can do it, you're expected to do it." So he told us, "First of all, you have to get false papers. Their police are all over the country, and the Germans—with their intelligence and their Gestapo—their police—they had to have identifications why you were at a certain place."

Today, what we're in right now, our army and the various arms—the navy—in Afghanistan, because of the situations that happened here in the United States, things are much tighter than they used to be. And it was very tight in Germany. You needed false papers. And he said there were people who were good forgers. They could make papers that you had to have. And you had to have civilian clothes, or something that wouldn't draw attention to you as a soldier. You couldn't wear your uniform. And it had to be organized in the camp. If you were in a stalag, you had to be able to have a committee to get you what you needed for the trip. Try to get some food that you could carry, find a compass, a map, a light, talk German. You have to have a watch, hide in daylight, possibly forage for food, travel at night when it's time to move, or to know what time of he day it is—you're away from clocks and everything—that you're going to be able to recognize some of the language so that if someone talks to you in German, you can try to catch some names of common words, etc. And it takes a lot of time and a lot of coordination. But when the time comes, it takes much delusion and things to do. Most stalags had roll call in the morning (really, a head count), so someone can move to cover for your absence. Possibly bribe some guard.

So, there was a man from the company I had been in, and we were over near Czechoslovakia. He was a non-commissioned officer, which most of us were over there. And when he was young, his family lived in Chicago. His father was engaged in international business. And this man had a sister, and he said, "My father used to come here and bring his family, and this man and his sister went to school here during peace-time. He used to come to Germany, and he had offices over here. We had a house to live in." And he said, "He would travel over to Germany with his family, come over in the summertime, and sometimes stay until later in the year and do his business over there and leave his office in Chicago." He said, "He took my mother, and my sister and me, and we came to Germany. Sometimes they would go earlier than they did others, and then we'd go to school for a while there, and then at other times, he would stay later, and we went to school." He said,"I learned to speak the language." So needs were provided for him, and they gave hm clothes and false papers. They found him a watch and a compass somewhere, so he could find his direction. He was pretty well acquainted with the overall geography of Germany, and he was somewhat familiar with the country where the stalag was. So he had a pretty good start.

Anyway, some men got him out of he stalag, and he was on his way. And of course, the next morning, when they took head count, there was some quick jumping around in the back. Anyway, he was gone for some time—I forgot how long. And one day, they brought him back. Sent him down to the barracks we were in. They gave him some kind of punishment—I don't know what it was. He came back, and I said to him, "You didn't quite make it?"

"No," he said, "I didn't quite make it. I did very well for

quite some time, but I came to a town that was on a river. There were large rocks and stuff down below where the river was, there was a hill on the other side of it, and the road went right straight through the town. It wasn't a real big place, but up until then, I was able to forage off the farms and stuff and sneak through. I pretty much traveled toward nighttime. But this day, I didn't want to try to crawl over those rocks down there at the river—or fall in that. It was too steep to climb part of the mountain that was there."

So he said he thought he'd wait until real early the next morning—like 3:00 or something, when it was dark and he didn't expect to find as many people out. So that's what he did.

He waited until 3:30, and he said he went through this town (and of course, everything was blacked out), and the town was quiet. He passed one person who was walking in the other direction. He was walking toward the west, and this stranger he passed was walking east. He said, "That's the only person I passed, and I didn't know that in this town, if you are traveling west, you walk on a certain side of the street, and if you're traveling east, you walk the other side. I was on the wrong side of the street. And when I got to the end, the Gestapo was sitting there waiting for me." He said they turned him over to the German army, and they brought him back. So escaping was a very difficult thing.

Now the British Air Force had some systems whereby they could recover their pilots who would get shot down out of fighter planes, or something, because it took so long to train a pilot. And they had special signals underground and everything, that they had worked out long years ago. And we hadn't got all that intelligence yet. So, no, I didn't escape. And furthermore, had I escaped, at every camp we were at, the Americans were far away at that time, and it was not knowing anything about the geography, nor having all the material and stuff to make it possible. A couple of men did try, but to try to get away was very difficult.

So anyway, one of the feelings that I had when we were there—now this was a mental feeling, and it was the idea of when I was there—I felt like I should get up and run away. It was a frustration. But that caused me some problems when I came home. My readjustment to civilian existence, I will talk about a little later. But I always felt that God was with me.